GW00691795

# —Words of—
# THANKS

Copyright © 1974 Lion Publishing

Published by
**Lion Publishing plc**
Icknield Way, Tring, Herts, England
ISBN 0 85648 305 2
**Albatross Books Pty Ltd**
PO Box 320, Sutherland, NSW 2232, Australia
ISBN 0 86760 211 2

First edition 1974, under the title *A Song of Praise*
Reprinted 1975, 1976, 1977, 1980, 1981, 1983,
1984 (twice), 1985, 1986

Photographs by Lion Publishing/David Alexander

Quotations from *Good News Bible,* copyright 1966,
1971 and 1976 American Bible Society; published
by Bible Societies/Collins

Printed and bound in Hong Kong

# Words of
# THANKS

# THANK YOU, LORD

I thank you, Lord, with all my heart;
I sing praise to you before the gods.
I bow down in front of your holy temple
and praise your name,
because of your constant love and faithfulness,
because you have shown that you and your
commands are supreme.
You answered me when I called to you;
with your strength you strengthened me.

All the kings of the earth will praise you, Lord,
because they have heard your promises.
They will sing about what the Lord has done,
and about his great glory.
Even though the Lord is so high above,
he cares for the lowly,
and the proud cannot hide from him.

*From* PSALM 138

In the village of Bethany, Jesus stayed in the humble
home of Martha, Mary and Lazarus.

# FAITHFUL AND JUST

Praise the Lord!

With all my heart I will thank the Lord,
in the meeting of his people.
How wonderful are the things the Lord does!
All who are pleased with them want to
understand them.
All he does is full of honour and majesty;
his righteousness is eternal . . .

In all he does he is faithful and just;
all his commandments are dependable.
They last for all time;
they were given in truth and righteousness.
He brought salvation to his people,
and made an eternal covenant with them.
Holy and mighty is he!
The way to become wise is to fear the Lord;
he gives sound judgement to all who obey
his commands.
He is to be praised for ever!

*From* PSALM III

The sun sets over a landscape in central Turkey.

# AS LONG AS I LIVE

Praise the Lord!
Praise the Lord, my soul!
I will praise him as long as I live;
I will sing to my God all my life.

Don't put your trust in human leaders,
or anyone else who cannot save you.
When they die they return to the soil;
on that day all their plans come to an end . . .

The Lord sets prisoners free
and gives sight to the blind.
He raises all who are humbled;
he loves his righteous people.
He protects the foreigners who live in the land;
he helps widows and orphans,
but ruins the plans of the wicked . . .

The Lord will be king for ever!
Your God, Zion, will reign for all time!

Praise the Lord!

*From* PSALM 146

Two girls look after the flock of sheep and goats near
Beersheba, Israel.

# HE GIVES ANIMALS THEIR FOOD . . .

Praise the Lord!

It is good to sing praise to our God;
it is pleasant and right to praise him . . .

He has determined the number of the stars
and calls each one by name.
Great and almighty is our Lord;
his knowledge cannot be measured.
He raises the humble,
but crushes the wicked to the ground.
Sing hymns of praise to the Lord;
play music to our God on the harp.
He spreads clouds over the sky;
he provides rain for the earth,
and makes grass grow on the hills.
He gives animals their food,
and feeds the young ravens when they call . . .

He takes pleasure in those who fear him,
in those who trust in his constant love . . .

Praise the Lord!

*From* PSALM 147

Cattle seek pasture amongst the rocks of Galilee.

# MY SAVIOUR

How I love you, Lord!
You are my defender.
The Lord is my Saviour;
he is my strong fortress.
My God is my protection,
and I am safe with him.
He protects me like a shield;
he defends me and keeps me safe.
I call to the Lord,
and he saves me from my enemies.
Praise the Lord!

*From* PSALM 18

The great walls and gates of the old city of Jerusalem.

# GOD'S FLOCK

Come, let us praise the Lord!
Let us sing for joy to our protector and
Saviour!
Let us come before him with thanksgiving,
and sing joyful songs of praise!
For the Lord is a mighty God,
a mighty king over all the gods.
He rules over the whole earth,
from the deepest caves to the highest hills.
He rules over the sea, which he made;
the land also, which he himself formed.

Come, let us bow down and worship him;
let us kneel before the Lord, our Maker!
He is our God;
we are the people he looks after,
the flock for which he provides.

*From* PSALM 95

A shepherd with his flocks beside the Lake of Galilee.

# GOD HAS HELPED ME

Give praise to the Lord;
he has heard my cry for help!
The Lord protects and defends me;
I trust in him.
He has helped me, and so I am glad
and sing hymns of praise to him.

The Lord protects his people;
he defends and saves his chosen king.
Save your people, Lord,
and bless those who are yours!
Be their shepherd,
and take care of them for ever.

*From* PSALM 28

A typical Middle Eastern street, with old and young.

# THIRST WILL BE SATISFIED

God, you are my God,
and I long for you.
My whole being desires you;
my soul is thirsty for you,
like a dry, worn-out, and waterless land.
Let me see you in the sanctuary;
let me see how mighty and glorious you are.
Your constant love is better than life itself,
and so I will praise you.
I will give thanks to you as long as I live;
I will raise my hands to you in prayer.
My soul will feast and be satisfied
and I will sing glad songs of praise to you.

*From* PSALM 63

A goat satisfies its thirst from the fresh water of the
Lake of Galilee.

# HOW GOOD THE LORD IS

I will always thank the Lord;
I will never stop praising him.
I will praise him for what he has done;
may all who are oppressed listen and be **glad**!
Proclaim with me the Lord's greatness;
let us praise his name together!

I prayed to the Lord, and he answered me;
he freed me from all my fears.
The oppressed look to him and are glad;
they will never be disappointed.
The helpless call to him, and he answers;
he saves them from all their troubles.
His angel guards those who fear the Lord
and rescues them from danger.

Find out for yourself how good the Lord is!
Happy is the man who finds safety with him!
Fear the Lord, all his people;
those who fear him have all they need.
Even lions lack food and go hungry,
but those who obey the Lord lack nothing
good.

*From* PSALM 34

Two riders on a track through the Syrian desert pass
an oasis of green trees.

# ALL NATIONS, ALL PEOPLES

Praise the Lord, all nations!
Praise him, all peoples!
His constant love for us is strong,
and his faithfulness is eternal.

Praise the Lord!

PSALM 117

Children play in the streets of the old city of Jerusalem.

# GOD SAVES

I waited and waited for the Lord's help;
then he listened to me and heard my cry.
He pulled me out of a dangerous pit,
out of a muddy hole!
He set me safely on a rock
and made me secure.
He taught me to sing a new song,
a song of praise to our God.
Many who see this will be afraid
and will put their trust in the Lord . . .

Lord, I know you will never stop being
merciful to me!
Your love and loyalty will always keep me
safe.

*From* PSALM 40

# GOD CARES

Praise the Lord!

You servants of the Lord,
praise his name!
His name will be praised,
now and for ever!
From the east to the west,
the Lord's name be praised!
The Lord rules over all nations,
his glory is above the heavens.

There is no one like the Lord our God;
he lives in the heights above,
but he bends down
to see the heavens and the earth.
He raises the poor from the dust;
he lifts the needy from their misery,
and makes them companions of princes,
the princes of his people.
He honours the childless wife in her home;
he makes her happy by giving her children.

Praise the Lord!

PSALM 113

A woman in rural Syria goes about her daily tasks.

# ALL LIVING THINGS

The Lord is faithful to his promises,
and good in all he does.
He helps all who are in trouble;
he raises all who are humbled.
All living things look hopefully to him,
and he gives them food when they need it.
He gives them enough
and satisfies the needs of all.
The Lord is righteous in all he does,
merciful in all his acts.
He is near to all who call to him,
who call to him with sincerity.
He supplies the needs of all who fear him;
he hears their cry and saves them.
He protects all who love him,
but he will destroy all the wicked.
I will always praise the Lord;
let all creatures praise his holy name for ever!

*From* PSALM 145

Storks are migrant visitors to Israel.

# PRAISE THE LORD, MY SOUL!

Praise the Lord, my soul!
All my being, praise his holy name!
Praise the Lord, my soul,
and do not forget how kind he is.
He forgives all my sins
and heals all my diseases;
he saves me from the grave
and blesses me with love and mercy;
he fills my life with good things,
so that I stay young and strong like an eagle . . .

The Lord set up his throne in heaven;
he is king over all.
Praise the Lord, you strong and mighty
angels,
who obey his commands,
who listen to what he says!
Praise the Lord, all you heavenly powers,
you servants who do what he wants!
Praise the Lord, all his creatures,
in every place he rules!
Praise the Lord, my soul!

*From* PSALM 103

Working the treadle of a traditional hand-loom in
the old city of Damascus.

# HOW GREAT YOU ARE!

We praise you, God, we praise you!
We proclaim how great you are,
and tell the wonderful things you have
done! . . .

Judgement does not come from the east or
from the west,
from the north or from the south;
it is God who does the judging,
putting some down and lifting others up.
The Lord holds a cup in his hand,
full of fresh wine, very strong;
he pours it out, and all the wicked drink it;
they drink it down to the last drop.

But I will never stop speaking of the God of
Jacob,
or singing praises to him.
He will break the power of the wicked,
but the power of the righteous will be
increased.

*From* PSALM 75

Behind the thorns, the sparkle of light gleaming on
water.

# WHY AM I TROUBLED?

Send your light and your truth;
may they lead me
and bring me back to Zion, your sacred hill,
and to your temple, where you live!
Then I will go to your altar, God,
because you give me joy and happiness;
I will play my harp and sing praise to you,
God, my God!

Why am I sad?
Why am I troubled?
I will put my hope in God,
and once again I will praise him,
my Saviour and my God.

*From* PSALM 43

Across the valley from the Temple area of Jerusalem,
these ancient olive-trees are in the Garden of
Gethsemane.

# THE GOD OF HISTORY

Give thanks to the Lord, proclaim his
greatness,
and make known to the nations what he has
done!
Sing to him, sing praise to him;
tell all the wonderful things he has done!
Be glad that we belong to him;
let all who serve the Lord rejoice!
Go to the Lord for help;
stay in his presence always.
You descendants of Abraham, his servant,
you descendants of Jacob, his chosen one:
remember his great and wonderful miracles,
and the judgements he gave . . .

Praise the Lord!

*From* PSALM 105

The moon above the mountains of Sinai, where
Israel received the law from God.

# THIS GOD IS OUR GOD

Inside your temple, God,
we think of your constant love.
You are praised by people everywhere,
and your fame extends over all the earth.
You rule with justice;
let the people of Zion be glad!
You give right judgements;
let there be joy in the cities of Judah!

Walk all round Mount Zion and count its
towers,
take notice of its walls, and examine its
fortresses,
so that you may tell the next generation
that this God is our God, for ever and ever;
he will lead us for all time to come.

*From* PSALM 48

# PRAISE HIM WITH HARPS

Praise the Lord!

Praise God in his temple!
Praise his strength in heaven!
Praise him for the mighty things he has done!
Praise his supreme greatness!

Praise him with trumpets!
Praise him with harps and lyres!
Praise him with drums and dancing!
Praise him with harps and flutes!
Praise him with cymbals!
Praise him with loud cymbals!
Praise the Lord, all living creatures!

Praise the Lord!

PSALM 150

A reconstruction in the Music Museum, Haifa, of
the type of harp used by David.

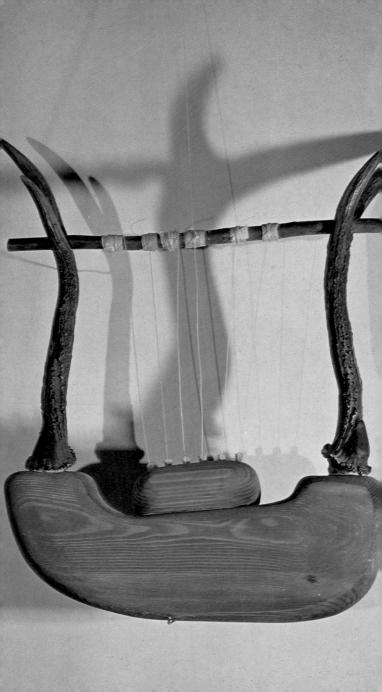

# PRAISE HIM, ALL THAT HE HAS MADE

Praise the Lord!

Praise the Lord from heaven,
you that live in the heights above!
Praise him, all his angels,
all his heavenly armies!

Praise him, sun and moon;
praise him, shining stars!
Praise him, highest heavens,
and the waters above the sky! . . .

Praise the Lord from the earth,
sea monsters and all ocean depths;
lightning and hail, snow and clouds,
strong winds that obey his command!

Praise him, hills and mountains,
fruit trees and forests;
all animals, tame and wild,
reptiles and birds!

Praise him, kings and all peoples,
princes and all other rulers;
young men and girls,
old people and children also!

Let them all praise the name of the Lord . . .

Praise the Lord!

*From* PSALM 148

The sun sinks behind the cedars of Lebanon.